Notes to Self

by

Laura Tansley

LIMITED EDITION OF 100
COPIES

TRICKHOUSE PRESS
LANCASTER
AUGUST 2021

Introduction

In November 2017, five or six months pregnant, I am making attempts to complete projects before my due date which has become a full-stop in my mind. What happens after this is impossible to know in so many ways – what will happen, how I will feel, or who I might be. The due date, a speculation in itself, has started to solidify into an unhelpful deadline in my thinking; a point at which I will have to submit and when creative work as I know it might be suspended, or perhaps permanently changed, perhaps for the worse. This terrifying prospect encourages me to place value on creative practice in a way I never have before – as something that is fundamental to me and my life. Something that I do not want to lose. I want to write, in whatever way I can in a post-pregnancy context, as a way to bridge the gap of the before and after that being a new mother is creating in my understanding of my self. It feels like a way to ensure that some of me will continue, that I will know something, even a small thing, after the baby is born. I consider the idea that by designing a specific creative practice in response to these growing feelings of concern, I might be able to leave a note to myself about the importance of writing, instructions to a future self about how to persist in the unknown afterwards.

Oulipean, but more organic & less arbitrary

I decide to make some presumptions about my experience of parenthood, and I create a creative practice around this. I decide that time, and how much of it I can dedicate to writing, to thinking, will be different, and so this new practice should foreground responsiveness over endless edits and the poring over of detail. I decide that this practice should encourage me to go outside, that it should be mobile, so I can leave my home and not feel caught inside it. I decide it should be an act that occurs in an instance, that captures a moment, because maybe that will be all I have to give, and as a consequence I have to acknowledge and accept that it might be inaccurate, misspelt, imperfect, which relieves myself from the pressure of product for the sake of continuing practice.

I create a kit: a pen and pencil, Post-it notes, a small notebook with blank pages. It all fits inside a purse that a good friend gave me, which fits inside my coat pocket. The purse has the slogan 'you ain't grabbing this pussy' emblazoned in pink glittery letters across its front. The times we live in. Later I find that it sits snuggly in the netted pouch of the pram I inherited from my brother and his children. The size of the Post-it notes gives me a spatial constraint; they are filled comfortably by a handful of words, and so they can be filled in fast and / or with focus. They also provide an in-progress context; they encourage a process-orientated approach because of the Post-it's position as marginalia, as opposed to main body. The notebook supports attempts, and is a place to archive the physical aspect of these pieces which I gather up and take with me once I'm done.

The Post-it notes, stationary I simply had lying around, become key to the creative act which functions as a kind of labelling, as a series of interventions or edits on existing scenes, exploring, and recording moments of categorisation: the remnants of a paper bag in a pile of brown leaves. A rotting onion in the road. The dropped, the left-behind, the lost. Each piece becomes a reminder as a way to remember, annotations and records of the ephemera and detritus of my surroundings, altered by my radically new reality. I fill a Post-it, place the note, take a picture on my phone to capture the scene I have created, then move on.

What I write about is whatever comes to mind; words or phrases that come when looking at the scene in front of me, but unquestionably informed by my child who is almost always present when these pieces are made. He is there in/directly, never pictured but ever present, until he contributes directly. 'His door' are his words, in response to a fly-tipped, unhinged pile at the top of Eastvale Place.

The consequences of this project are a sense of being able to carry a part of a previous self into a new state of being, the comfort of this, and the capacity to carry on. The result of bringing these pieces together is a specific record of my experience of pregnancy and new parenthood; behind each of these pieces I am romantic, I am amazed by myself, and I am also leaking, terrified, and sometimes desperate.

As I write this, I am pregnant again, conscious of the next new reality fast approaching, and curious about what parts of myself will persist through this next afterwards; what kind of self might emerge, what I can carry, what and how I can continue, what reminders, lists, inventories I need to catalogue and create, to keep the parts of me that have been, or have become, so important.

-Glasgow, May 2021

Context (On Cranes)

Do Not Assume (On Fallen Blossom)

Weight

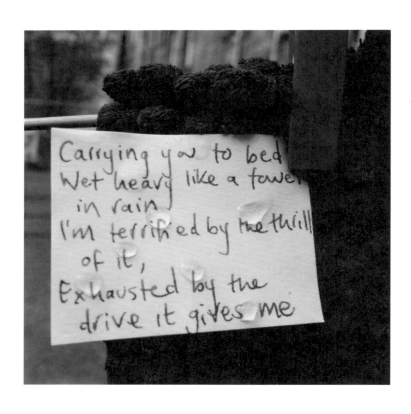

Y/our Potential (On a Sprouting Brick)

Strawberry Crush

Fatigue

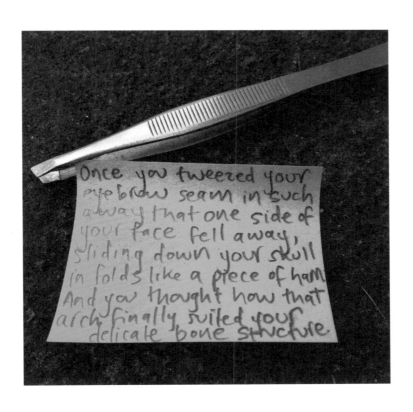

Your Hand

Your guarded hand is the
size of a garden bird
scruffed up with fright
from flying into its own
reflection. That's why
whenever we're out for
walks I avoid taking you
too close to water.

Transition and Retention
(On Leaver's Ribbons)

1

on the last
day of
school
scores of us
sucked love
bites on to
our arms
to see

The cadbury coloured bruises sank back into us but the feeling of a moist mouth lasted like a sprain.

Sheltering

My idea of shelter
is a fat leaf, the
kind that amplifies
the sounds of
atmospherics; or
a caravan roof;
or a rain cover;
or a flat handed
salute shading eyes
from the sun.

Breathing Space

ONE SIZE

MADE IN CHINA

If there is only one
fit then we're all
out of shape, all have
the same dimensions.
Ubiquity is the smell of
of a wet woollen glove
held too close to your mouth.

Motion Sickness

Waving Back

After Birth

Possibilities

Sympathetic Camouflage (On a Paper Bag)

Postpartum Hair

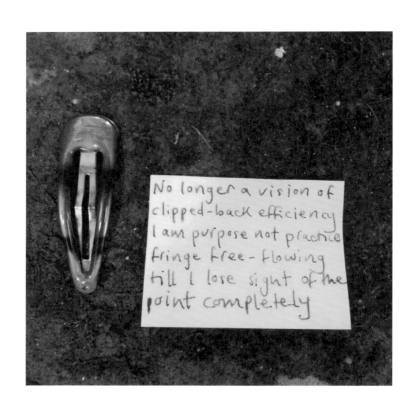

No longer a vision of
clipped-back efficiency
I am purpose not practice
fringe free-flowing
till I lose sight of the
point completely

Rip It Up and Start Again

Baby Brain or Lighten the Word
(On a Lampshade)

Domestic Chores

Oh I'm grounded alright. Well & truly. I dance for joy at the thought of all your problems. Re-birth myself in twisted wires like ribbons round a Maypole

To Be Seen, To Blend In (On a Banana Skin)

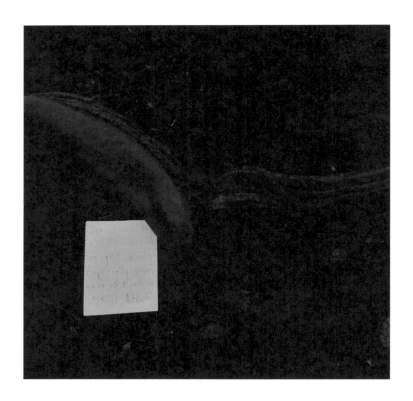

Dressing the Part
(On a Suit Jacket with Slug Slime)

Reveal

it's weird &
quite funny that I'm getting mad
at this bork because of the
tone of voice i'm reading it in.

Cover Up

When we discussed
redecorating did you
mean a cleansing
lick? A white renewal?
Or a good pasting, a
brushing in to
submission?

Going in Blind

Oxidise

Drain(ing)

Frayed

His Door

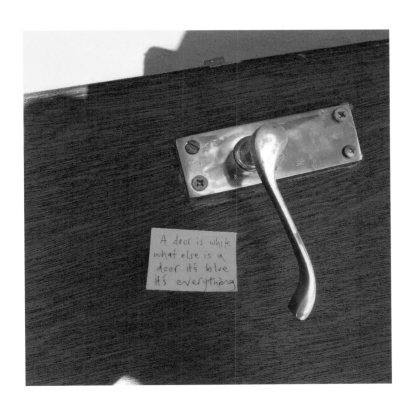

Inherit

The tradition in his family is to suddenly need glasses after turning Thirty. The view for me gets skewed when he decides its inevitable and wears a pair anyway, starts talking about the economy

Needs (On a Tree-Caught Kite)

L/edge (On Drying Trainers)

To share as little space as possible is to know how magnets work; how nests are built; how a minute moment in a colour spectrum catches us at the very edge of our peripheries.

The Sustaining Body

Oh Boy

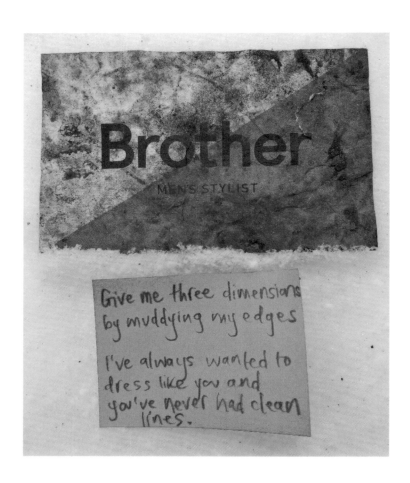

Pushing A Pull

Body Swap

What's Mine to Give